# Jonah

## The Pursuing Love and Grace of God

By Effie Darlene Barba

Cover photo titled "Lord in my Pain, I see Your Blessing" used by

permission of RoninRon's Custom Art. The original may be found

on RoninRon.com. Or you may contact the artist at

Contact@roninron.com

Unless otherwise noted, scripture is from the King James Version

Bible

## Dedication

I dedicate this book to my three children, Melissa Smith, Ronald Barba, and Alberto Barba. Truly they are symbols of God's Grace toward me, for I did not deserve such favor as to have been blessed with their love in my life. Still God gave me His best when He allowed me to be their mother.

# Contents

# I Turned and Saw the Face of God

By Effie Darlene Barba

I turned and saw the Face of God

His Glory did surround me

He smiled and gave a wink, a nod

No chaos could confound me


His Grace and Mercy were now mine

His Joy was Mine Abounding

That I might then His Glory shine

And shout His praise resounding

x

# Introduction

The book of Jonah is unique among the books of prophecy. There are only nine "prophetic" words spoken by the prophet within the book of Jonah; yet, this book clearly tells the story of God's pursuing love and Grace toward Jonah, Israel and to all of mankind. God pursues us with a relentless love, desiring that all would come to Him (I Timothy 2:4; 2 Peter 3:9; Ezekiel 18:23; Matthew 23:37). He is Sovereign and could command it to be so; however, He knows if He did that, no longer would that be true love. Were He not to allow individuals the free will to love Him, well we would not understand or know what true love is. Instead we would be robots without thought or emotion. Before time began, He knew those who would accept His gift of Grace and those who reject Him. Yet, He pursues every human heart with an unshakable love. That is the story of Jonah.

Rather than to prophecy of Israel's future, it tells the story of a moment in the life of Jonah, the prophet. Despite that being true, it is the book that is read near the end of the Jewish fast of Yom Kippur each year. Yom Kippur meaning "Day of Atonement" is the most solemn religious fast of the Jewish year. It is the last day of the ten days of penitence that begins with Rosh Hashanah.

So, why would the Jewish nation choose Jonah as the book to read at such an important festival? After all, Jonah tells of God's grace to a gentile nation, the Ninevites rather than directly toward the Jewish nation. Furthermore, the Ninevites were known for their barbaric cruelty, their hatred of the Jewish nation, and their idolatrous lifestyle. The Ninevites reputation stands as one of the evilest nations to have ever lived. They were feared for their tactics of burying people alive in the sand with only their head exposed and then nailing their tongues to the ground where they were left to die a slow and grueling death. And this was considered one of their lesser evils. An idolatrous nation, they certainly did not acknowledge Jehovah, the one true God. Human sacrifice was a common occurrence within their "religious rituals".

Furthermore, Jonah was not a humble obedient prophet, praying for God's mercy upon His people. Instead Jonah, was as strong willed and disobedient as the people of Israel during that time. His prophetic words within the book of Jonah are limited to only one sentence: "Yet forty days, and Nineveh shall be overthrown" (Jonah 3:4).[1] Still, the book of Jonah accomplishes its prophetic message to Israel and Judah, by example, through telling a historical story from the life of the prophet Jonah. The desperate pleas and prayers of other prophets for the people of Israel and Judah all too often fell on deaf ears. Yet, Jonah in his honest portrayal of himself, also told the story of his own

---

[1] Biblical References: Unless otherwise noted, all Biblical passages referenced are in the King James Version

people's rebellious disobedience of God, their arrogance, and the mockery of grace their lives portrayed.

The nation of Israel and Judah had ignored the warnings of the prophet. They took God's grace for granted, as though owed to them regardless of their behavior. Meanwhile, these few words spoken to one of the evilest, gentile nations to walk upon the earth lead to the repentance and salvation of the people of Nineveh. It remains a searing rebuke to the nation of Israel as well as to we who proclaim to be the followers of Christ.

The prophet Jonah certainly was not praying for a revival. In fact, when revival came instead of rejoicing, Jonah was angry. He was furious with

God and wanted to die, right then and there, rather than to accept the truth that God showed grace, love and mercy to these people whom he believed so unworthy. Never did he consider for a moment his own unworthiness at the time. What he saw as an unfulfilled prophecy was presented by an unwilling prophet to a gentile nation. Why then does the book of Jonah stand out as a book for the ages? Why would it be chosen as the Prophet to be read during Yom Kippur? Within the opening commentary of the Liberty Study Bible is presented this case.

> The purpose of Jonah's prophecy is to show the sovereignty of God at work in the life of an individual (the prophet Jonah), and his (God's) concern for a heathen nation (Assyria). The prophecy also shows, in an oblique way, his concern for His own people and that the way to avert national

catastrophe is a concentrated missionary effort toward all people.[2]

Furthermore, it demonstrates God's love and desire that all sinners come to know Him, truly repenting and turning from their sin. God's love cries forth to all who are lost; bidding them to come to a saving knowledge of Him by acknowledging, repenting and turning from their sin.

Jonah in his response to God demonstrated the pride and arrogance of the self-righteous, who fail to see that it is grace and grace alone that saves. Jonah's story went much deeper than just the salvation of the people of Nineveh by God's grace. It shone forth God's glory in His relentless pursuit

---

[2] Jerry Falwell, ed., *The Liberty Annotated Study Bible,* (Nashville, TN: Thomas Nelson, 1988), 1329.

of Jonah, His Grace that reached out to an undeserving servant, and His ultimate victory in transforming Jonah's heart.

Additionally, it was a warning and admonition to an unrepentant Jewish nation who blatantly mocked God's grace, by living lives filled with idolatry and sin. Unless they also truly repented of their sins, turning from them, they would surely face judgement; because, their hearts were filled with evil. Furthermore, they had failed in the commission God had given them to represent Him to a lost and dying world by both word and deed. God set forth to accomplish what He had commissioned Israel to do.

Jonah was addressed to Israel as noted by John D. Hannah. "The book was written not simply to record a historical narrative; in addition, it conveyed a message to the Northern Kingdom."[3] Israel had been called out to live as a people who displayed God's Glory to all the nations (Isaiah 49:3). But alas, they had failed. Chasing after idolatry, pride, violence, adultery, lust, and riches; they presented no evidence of God's Glory. Neither did they listen to the many prophets sent to them. "Nineveh's repentance contrasted sharply with Israel's rejection of the warning of Jonah's contemporaries, Hosea and Amos."[4] God, often

---

[3] John D. Hannah, "Jonah", *The Bible Knowledge Commentary:* John Walvoord and Roy Zuck, eds., (Colorado Springs: CO: Victor, 2004), 1462

[4] Hannah, "Jonah", 1462.

allowed the life of his prophets also to be a part of their message, such as the death of Ezekiel's wife, Hosea's unfailing love and care for a wayward wife who shunned him for a life of prostitution, or Daniel who shined forth his faith as a captive. So, it is no mystery that God used the unwillingness of Jonah to demonstrate to a rebellious nation, that God will ultimately accomplish His will in their life and that of the nation of Israel, even if that means He will justly send them into exile and some will face eternity apart from His Grace; because, they choose to not follow Him. Even though God pursues them relentlessly, many will run away from His love and His Grace, seeking after that which can never fully satisfy the longings of their heart.

To study the book of Jonah, we will begin with a deeply exegetical commentary of the book. This will be followed with significant applications from the book of Jonah. So, pull up a seat, lean back and let's study the book of Jonah together.

# Historical Background and Prevailing Conditions

The Northern Kingdom including the ten tribes of Israel (Asher, Dan, Ephraim, Gad, Issachar, Manasseh, Naphtali, Reuben, Simeon, and Zebulun) were politically divided from Judah (consisting of the tribe of Judah and Benjamin). This division had been in place since 931 B.C. In fact, Israel and Judah were at times rivals and even enemies, rather than standing together as one nation under God. Jonah was a prophet during the reign of Jeroboam II from 793-753 B.C. who ruled over the Northern Kingdom. As John MacArthur describes, Israel "enjoyed a time of relative peace and prosperity...Spiritually, however, it was a time of spiritual poverty; religion was ritualistic and increasingly idolatrous, and justice became perverted. Peacetime and wealth had made her bankrupt spiritually, morally, and ethically (cf. 2 Kings 14:24, Amos 4:1, 5:10-13)"[5]

The Assyrians had previously attacked Israel and received tribute from Jehu, king of Israel sometime within the years of 859 and 824 B.C.[6] They were enemies of Israel. Assyrians were equally feared and hated by both the northern and the southern tribes of the Jewish nation. Furthermore, as Sheri Klouda writes: "Nineveh was the capital city of Assyria, whose people enjoyed a

---

[5] John MacArthur, *The MacArthur Bible Commentary,* (Nashville, TN: Thomas Nelson, 2005), 1006.
[66] Hannah, "Jonah", 1463.

reputation for their severe cruelty, especially toward Israel. Often, they impaled their captives or wore amulets around their necks created from human heads."[7]

Yet, we will find that God loved the Ninevites, desiring that they come to a saving knowledge of Himself. Through natural disasters, God had been preparing their hearts even before He sent Jonah. History shows that the Assyrians had suffered two foreboding famines in 765 B. C. and 759 B.C., as well as a total solar eclipse on June 15, 763[8]; thereby, preparing their hearts to receive Jonah's message.

---

[7] Sheri Klouda, "Jonah", In *Baker Illustrated Bible Commentary,* by Gary M. Burge and Andrew E. Hill, 2nd ed., (Baker Publishing Group, 2012), Historical Context.
[8] Sheri Klouda, "Jonah", 1464.

# Main Character

The story tells of Jonah, the son of Amittai. "Although the text never mentions Jonah as the author, both Jewish and Christian traditions attribute authorship of the book to the eighth-century-BC prophet Jonah mentioned in 2 Kings 14:25."[9] Rabbi Steven Bob in discussing the significance of Jonah's name wrote: "Jonah in the original Hebrew is Yonah. Yonah means "dove," and the word is used in the Noah story in Genesis 8...the dove represents the possibility of a new beginning"[10] In Jonah 1:1, we are also told that he

---

[9] Ibid., Authorship and Date

[10] Steven Bob, *Jonah and the Meaning of Our Lives: A Verse-by-Verse Contemporary Commentary,* (The Jewish Publication Society, 2016), 1-2

15

is the son of Amittai. "Amittai derives from the Hebrew word emet, which means truth. Jonah then is the son of truth."[11] From 2 Kings 14:25, we also learn that he is a prophet from Gathhepher. Furthermore, he had prophesied accurately that King Jeroboam of Israel would expand the borders of his kingdom; leading to the prosperity and peace previously mentioned.

Since, the entire book is written in third person; some want to say that Jonah was not the author. However, many of the Old Testament writers did write in third person. Furthermore, given that the book ends with a discouraged prophet under God's rebuke, the reader would also be

---

[11] Ibid.,2

discouraged; "but because it is written in the third person the reader knows that the prophet wrote it after he had returned" home and favorably responded to God's rebuke.[12] Of note, Rabbi Bob points out that in the Midrash (the early Jewish commentary), Jonah is thought to be the widow's son raised from the dead by Elijah in I Kings 17:19-22 and the disciple of Elisha sent to anoint Jehu as King in 2 Kings 9:1-3.

With all that, one would think Jonah is the main character; however, he is not. God is the main character in the book of Jonah. God's power is displayed as He hurled a great wind upon the sea, His sovereignty shines as He commands the fish,

---

[12] Falwell, *Liberty,* 1329

His mercy is revealed as He recommissions an unwilling prophet, His grace shines bright as He accepts the repentance of the Ninevites and the sailors, His patience is displayed as He teaches Jonah, and His love shines brightly throughout the entire book: displayed in His compassion for the people of Nineveh, the sailors, and Jonah. All in all, God's Character and Glory is clearly on display and He is the main Character in the book of Jonah.

## Major Argument

There is no greater thing but that every person obeys God, trusting Him with the consequences; because, He is a God of righteousness, justice, mercy, and pursuing, boundless love.

# Major Themes

1. God is sovereign.

2. The love of God reaches out to all people.

3. God can even use a reluctant, despairing prophet to do His will.

4. Never is God taken by surprise.

5. God always has a plan to complete His task, His way.

6. God will accomplish all that He has planned.

7. Each individual person must face the consequences of disobeying God.

8. The mercy and patience of God is boundless.

9. God's plan is always best.

10. God's Pursuing Love is relentless.

11. God's All-encompassing love is greater than our prejudices.

12. A broken and contrite heart, God will not despise (Psalm 51:17).

13. God will transform the heart of those who seek Him, whatever it takes.

14. We are called to spread the gospel to all people, even our enemies.

Leslie Allen wrote: "A Jonah lurks in every Christian heart, whimpering his insidious message of smug prejudice, empty traditionalism, and exclusive solidarity."[13]

---

[13] Leslie Allen, *The Books of Joel, Obadiah, Jonah and Micah. (The New International Commentary on the Old Testament),* eds. R. K. Harrison and Robert Hubbard, Jr. (Grand Rapids, MI: Wm B. Eerdsmans Publishing, 1976), 235.

# Outline

1.  Varying Responses to God's Call (1:1-17)

    1.1 Running from God (1:1-3)

    1.2 God Sends a Storm (1:4-6)

    1.3 Guilty as Charged (1:7-13)

    1.4 Believing They Pray (1:14-16)

    1.5 God Sends a Fish to Rescue (1:17)

2.  Salvation Belongs to the Lord (2:1-10)

    2.1 A Woeful Cry (2:1-2)

    2.2  Separated from God's Presence (2:3-5)

    2.3 Sorrow Turns to Praise (2:6-9)

    2.4 God Answers (2:10)

3.  God's Grace on Display: Second Chances (3:1-10)

    3.1 God Calls Jonah Again (3:1-2)

    3.2 An Obedient Servant (3:3-4)

    3.3 Revival Comes to Nineveh (3:5-10)

4.  Lessons from God (4:1-11)

# Varying Responses to God's Call

## (Chapter 1)

Jonah receives a direct command from God to "Arise, go to Nineveh, that great city, and cry against it; for their wickedness is come up before me" (Jonah 1:2). The Hebrew word for arise "qūm" was used by God often preceding a significant command. It was the command He gave to Abraham (Genesis 13:17), Lot (Genesis 19:15), Jacob (Genesis 28:2, 31:15, 35:1), Joshua (Joshua 1:2, 7:10, 7:13), and Jeremiah (Jeremiah 13:6, 18:2). So, this command was not of any minor consequence. Jonah knew this to be the case. God used it to command one to move from their state of inaction to go and do whatever God commanded.

Yet, in Jonah's case the state of inaction depicted Jonah's heart as much as his life's work. This command always came with promise if followed or consequences if not. Therefore, one would have expected Jonah to "rise up and go to Nineveh". Yet, instead he rose up and fled to Tarshish.

Nineveh was the capital city of the Assyrian Empire, located about 550 miles northeast of Israel. On several occasions, God referred to Nineveh as a great city. John MacArthur wrote: "Nineveh was great both in size and in power, exerting significant influence over the Middle East…magnificent walls almost eight miles long enveloped the inner city, with the rest of the city/district occupying an area with a circumference of some sixty miles."[14]  They were known for their worship of the fish goddess Nanshe and Dagon the fish god.  Furthermore, they were known as a cruel empire who had previously attacked Israel, as was pointed out in the introduction. Of all the nations they were believed to be the most demonically evil people of their time.

As John Hannah wrote:

> "Though Jonah apparently understood and appreciated God's wrath against Assyria, he was not nearly so compassionate as God was. Motivated by patriotic duty that clouded religious obligation, and knowing God's forgiving mercy, Jonah shirked his responsibility. It is strange that a prophet of God would not follow God's command to preach condemnation."[15]

---

[14] MacArthur, *Bible Commentary,* 1008.
[15] Hannah, "Jonah", 1465

Jonah was the only prophet sent forth to preach directly to a gentile nation. Unless, of course, you consider Daniel who prophesied while in Babylon to King Nebuchadnezzar. The only other prophecy we have recorded by Jonah had been one of prosperity to King Jeroboam II; despite King Jeroboam II having done evil in the sight of the Lord (2 Kings 14:25). Therefore, Jonah was possibly known in his time, "as a *feel-good* prophet." At least it appears, he was content with his work as such and wanted his reputation to stand intact.

## Running from God (1:3)

Instead of doing what God commanded, Jonah decided to catch a boat at Joppa to take him to Tarshish. "The location of Tarshish, famous for its wealth (Ps. 72:10, Jer. 10:9; Ezek. 27: 12,25), is not known for certain. "The Greek historian Herodotus identified it with Tartessus, a merchant city in Southern Spain."[16] Tartessus was about 2500 miles in the opposite direction to where Jonah was being sent.

Why would Jonah run away from God? There could be many reasons. As suggested by Rabbi Bob, he might have been afraid for his life.[17] After all, despite many prophets pronouncing God's coming judgement on evil gentile nations, no other prophet was asked to go. Of course, there was Daniel who stood out as God's witness in Babylon years later; but, he was taken captive by the

---

[16] MacArthur, *Bible Commentary*, 1008
[17] Bob, *Jonah*, 15

Babylonians, rather than being commanded to go to them. Furthermore, God wasn't sending an army with Jonah to protect him, He just said, "go." Although, in truth, fear of death appears unlikely as his motive, given his willingness to be thrown overboard and his death wishes in Chapter 4.

However, in Jonah 4:2; lies another clue as to his disobedience, when Jonah says, "for I knew that thou art a gracious God, and merciful, slow to anger, and of great kindness." So, Jonah saw the Ninevites as undeserving of mercy. Furthermore, did he, as suggested in the midrash, feel that it was better to die at sea than to disgrace the Israeli nation.[18] His arrogance, hatred of the Ninevites, and self-

---

[18] Bob, *Jonah,* 15

centeredness mirrored that of the Israeli nation. He, nor the nation, recognized that they were no more deserving of God's grace than the Ninevites. They had taken God's grace for granted, as though they deserved it. Instead of bowing humbly before God in praise and worship for all He had done, they saw God's protection and provision as some right they were entitled to have regardless of their response.

## God Hurls a Storm (1:4-6)

This is not some ordinary storm. Several translations such as the New American Standard Bible, New Living Translation or the English Standard version all translate this as, "The Lord hurled a great wind upon the sea". It was enough to make the seasoned sailors fear for their life (v. 5).

All of them began to pray to whatever pagan god they could think of. Finally, they go down and awaken the sleeping runaway to ask him to pray to whatever God he believed in; because, theirs were not responding. As John Hannah pointed out, "The need was so great that they despaired for their lives; yet, God's servant slept. What an object lesson to God's people then and now to awaken from apathy as crying people perish on the sea of life."[19]

We see again, in verse 6 of chapter 1 that Jonah is commanded to arise. This time it is by the shipmaster who commanded that he arise and pray. Jonah once more rose up; but, there is no indication that he prayed to God, as was the second part of this

[19] Hannah, "Jonah", 1466

command. In other words, he rose up and once more attempted to run from God's presence rather than to seek God's presence.

## Guilty as Charged (1:7-13)

Then, of course the sailors do the next logical thing to help. Believing that this horror must be due to the wrath of some god, they cast lots to determine who infuriated the gods. Naturally, by God's providence and Sovereignty, "the lot fell on Jonah" (1:7). Immediately, they wanted to know what horrible thing he had done to bring such anger from whatever god was causing this. Jonah in verse 9 tells them, "I am a Hebrew; and I fear the Lord, the God of heaven, which hath made the sea and the dry land." This certainly did not make sense to these sailors. After all, if Jonah feared God and God controlled the seas; why would Jonah have run from Him onto a boat in the sea?

Jonah's confession, of course, made the men more afraid than ever. Now they were confronted with a runaway prophet, who confesses that he was running away from God and this God was so powerful as to "hurl a violent wind" so strong as to nearly break their boat in pieces. They most likely wondered amongst each other, why had they even allowed this stowaway to join them without asking him more questions before his boarding their ship. So, next, they ask Jonah what to do to appease his God, so the sea could be calm (v 11). He tells them to pick him up and throw him into the sea; because, "for my sake, this great tempest is upon you" (1:12).

That was even more terrifying to the sailors, who then tried with all their might to row to shore. If, indeed Jonah was a holy man and they tossed him into the sea; what, would his God do to them? They were witness to God's power and they feared Him. Pagan worship often did involve human sacrifices. Normally they would not have thought anything of sacrificing Jonah; however, this time their conscience was telling them otherwise. As Klouda writes: "The narrative hints at the concept of human sacrifice as a means of appeasing the sea god and depicts the sailors as morally upright in seeking other alternatives. It is interesting to note that while

Jonah seems unaware of the conflict facing the sailors, he does not find anything wrong with the request."[20] Therefore, the response of the sailors appeared to have even more significance. Suddenly, their hearts were transforming, and they did not think a human sacrifice could appease the one true God who ruled over the seas. Had they heard of the Hebrew God before?

## Believing They Pray (v. 14-16)

Throughout this scene, there is no recorded prayer by Jonah. However, the sailors begin to pray to God and call Him, "Lord". They acknowledge that the Lord is responsible for the storm and now

---

[20] Klouda, *Baker Bible Commentary,* "The Sailor's Response to Crisis at Sea"

they ask that He protect them. Then they also ask that the blood of Jonah not be charged on them; because, they believe God has done this. Immediately, after throwing Jonah overboard, the sea calms and the sailors begin to make vows to God and "offer sacrifices unto the Lord" (1:16).

Note that despite Jonah's disobedience, his arrogance, his belief that gentiles were undeserving of grace, and even, his failure to pray for these sailors whom he had placed in peril; God led the sailors to a repentant, genuine faith in Himself. A true picture of God's Sovereignty, Grace, Power, Love, and Glory regardless of Jonah. At any point Jonah could have repented and been used as a part of that miracle. Despite Jonah not being a willing participant, God accomplished His plan of salvation for these sailors through Jonah. Jonah's rebellious attitude never took God by surprise and God had a plan of redemption for Jonah, Nineveh and the sailors. Jonah would still face the consequences of his disobedience; because, God still had a plan to transform the heart of Jonah, thus truly saving him. But for the moment, instead of celebrating in the overflowing joy that sinners were saved by grace, Jonah continued in his own selfish misery.

**God Sends a Fish to Rescue (1:17)**

Just as Jonah is cast into the water, the sea grows calm. Jonah, instead of drowning, is swallowed up by a "great fish". There are some who may say, this is impossible and just a "story" added. Others say that God created a special fish just to swallow up Jonah. However, as the Liberty Bible commentary points out: "prepared indicates 'to appoint, ordain, prepare, or order.' The idea is one of commission rather than of creation."[21] God is sovereign over all the creatures of the land, sky, and sea. For those skeptics, Jesus spoke of Jonah having spent three days and three nights in the belly of the great fish in Matthew 12:40. Obviously, the fish was more obedient than Jonah. Yet, as Leslie Allen wrote: "The gracious gift of God is life. He does not abandon his servant to death but snatches from its clutches the drowning man."[22]

---

[21] Falwell, *Liberty*, 1331.
[22] Allen, *Jonah*, 213.

God's Sovereignty is on display throughout the book of Jonah. He is Sovereign over the storm. Miraculously, He brings about the salvation of the sailor's eternity as well as their life here on earth. The sea, the wind and the great fish immediately obey His commands. There was no detail or circumstance, that He did not allow and ordain. That same truth remains steadfast today. Whatever circumstance you may be facing, God is ultimately Sovereign over every detail. His greatest desire is to transform the hearts of men and women, so they might desire Him above all else.

## Salvation Belongs to the Lord (Chapter 2)

Alive in the belly of the great fish, Jonah prays for the first time in this story. One might think, his first words would be, "Thank you, Lord," or a word of praise. Yet, Jonah seems to be preoccupied with self and his feelings; much, like the nation of Israel for whom he was a prophet. He does get around to praising God for having saved his life by sending the fish to swallow him; however, he opens his prayer recounting his near-death experience in the swirling water. There is no mention of repentance on the part of Jonah in this prayer; although, he does end the prayer with a promise to worship and praise God for his salvation.

This prayer is in the form of a poem. Most would say that given its poetic format, it was composed many years later and did not reflect the actual words that were prayed. However, as a poet, I must say that often my poetry comes from a place of grave emotional distress. The words form with a raw vulnerability, searching for an answer that comes as I focus on God alone for the answer. Poems were used throughout Israel's history to hold fast the truth of their experience in worship. The poetic form was often used to etch and memorize the truth of a situation. Therefore, I believe that this is the prayer etched in permanent ink within the mind of Jonah; rather than being written later.

## A Woeful Cry (2:1-2)

Jonah cried out to God, "by reason of my affliction" …"out of the belly of hell" (2:2). As we were already told, he had not literally died nor was he in hell. This was hyperbolic language from the depth of his emotion. He had nearly died. When he recognized the peril, he for the first time in the story, turned to God and cried out for help. Realizing he had no one else to turn to, he cried to God for help and God sent a big fish to swallow him, saving him from drowning in the depth of the sea. Finally, Jonah saw God as the only one who could help him, and he turned to seek God's help. Perhaps, not fully repentant yet; but, a step in the right direction to recognize that God was Sovereign over his life, as well as the Universe, and able to save.

## Separated from God's Presence (2:3-5)

He cries out with despair at having felt cast out by God, separated from His presence. Fully recognizing, that it was God, not the sailors, who had thrust him into the sea where he felt abandoned and alone. Yet, as though he remembers God's grace that sent the fish to save him from the raging sea, Jonah realizes that God had not abandoned him. Whatever he felt of loneliness and separation from God, he would look toward the holy temple of God.

Jesus was thrown into the center of God's wrath; because, of His love for us and to atone for our rebellion. We, who like Jonah, run from God as far as we can. Seeking to find pleasure and happiness apart from Him, we run to the farthest shores. Yet, the true storm of God's wrath, was hurled upon His perfect righteous Son.

For a moment in time, when all our guilt and shame were laid upon His shoulders, the Father and the Holy Spirit turned their back. The earth grew black as Christ cried out, "My God, My God why hast thou forsaken me" (Mark 15:34). He bore the loneliness of abandonment by God for us. We deserve eternal abandonment by God. Yet, all the wrath of God against sin was poured out on Him, that we might be saved from our sins and clothed in His righteousness forever, if only we would repent and accept His gift of salvation through faith.

## Sorrow Turns to Praise (2:6-9)

Jonah begins his prayer in verse 6 once more with describing the depth of his separation from God. Herein, Jonah returns to describing his entrapment within the sea prior to the fish swallowing him. It is with detail, he speaks of his encounter. "the depth closed me round about, the weeds were wrapped about my head." (Jonah 2:5). Have you dear Christian ever felt the weeds of sin entangling your mind and heart as the depth of this world closes around you? Then, dear one, read on for God has a plan to save you from the depth of the drowning sea you may find yourself in.

Jonah's prayer takes a turn ¾ of the way through verse 6, where suddenly Jonah prays, "yet hast thou brought up my life from corruption, O Lord my God." He goes on to pray that when his soul had fainted, he remembered the Lord.

As though amazed by the thought that God heard him from His Holy Temple. Even further, he suddenly says, "they that observe lying vanities forsake their own mercy." (2:8). This may have been a confession of his own guilt of selfish pride and vanity or as the NIV translates it, a denouncement of idol worship. Either way, it is as though a lightbulb went off in his own mind; reminding Jonah that he, alone was guilty of forsaking the mercy God had afforded him. Then finally in verse 9, he offers a voice of thanksgiving. He reaches the conclusion of it all. "Salvation is of the Lord" (Jonah 2:9). That is when God answers him fully by releasing him from the captivity of the great fish.

This would be an important lesson for Israel who had come to rely on many false gods for their protection and their prosperity. They had abandoned the only true God. Although, they continued the rituals of worship, they had abandoned true worship. Unless, they repented and turned their hearts and mind to God; they too, would be forced into exile where they would face the feelings of abandonment, fear, desperation, and loneliness that Jonah had.

For a moment, Jonah had come to the end of himself.  Although, we shall see that this is not yet complete surrender, as self will rise again to take the throne in Jonah's life.  However, it was a step in the right direction.  He boldly declared, "I will sacrifice unto thee with the voice of thanksgiving; I will pay that that I have vowed" (Jonah 2:10).

Much like Jonah, we vow to God our unswerving devotion amid our storms in life. "God, if you would save me now from these wretched circumstances; I will praise and worship you." Thank God, for His patient endurance, His steadfast love and unwavering pursuit of us.

## God Answers

God speaks to the fish. The fish follows God's request and vomits Jonah onto dry land. "Just as God spoke the world into existence (Gen. 1:3, 6, 9,11, 14 20, 24) and calls the stars by name, so He speaks to His creation in the animal world."[23]

---

[23] MacArthur, *Bible Commentary,* 1011

## God's Grace and Second Chances (Chapter 3)

Jonah was dumped by God onto the shores of Joppa after his attempt to run from God's command. Actually, the fish vomited him up on shore at God's command. Now God gives Jonah a second chance to obey. Certainly, God could have chosen a different prophet; but, He did not. There is no indication that God verbally criticized or demeaned Job; instead, He repeats His command with precision and clarity. Furthermore, as chapter 3 unfolds; God also gives the inhabitants of Nineveh a second chance. God's grace is displayed throughout chapter 3 of Jonah, demonstrating His love and desire that all men be saved, whatever their background.

There is a parallel demonstrated between the way that the sailors came to acknowledge God and the way that the Ninevites came to repentance. The sailors faced impending doom in Jonah 1:4, when God thrust a wind upon the sea. In Jonah 3:4, God proclaims impending disaster. Just as God's judgement is universal, so is His mercy and grace upon all who would truly repent and turn to Him, proclaiming Him as Lord. God's judgement and God's grace are not dependent upon social class, race, or nationality. All are guilty before an Almighty, Holy God and all are offered His gift of grace, if they will truly repent and seek Him for salvation. There is no one so righteous as to not need a Savior and no one so wicked to not be saved if only they come humbly in faith.

## God Calls Jonah Again (3:1-2)

Once more "the word of the Lord came unto Jonah...Arise, go unto Nineveh, that great city" (Jonah 3:1-2). Again, God refers to Nineveh as a great city. Certainly, from God's vantage point, the largest city ever built would be less than a speck of sand compared to the Universe. However, as Leslie Allen points out, three times God refers to it as "that great city" (1:2, 3:2, 4:11). Thus, the city of Nineveh was "great to God,"[24]referring to more than just its size. It certainly was great regarding its political positioning, its fortified walls, and cultural advancement. Yet, would any of that make it great

---

[24] Allen, *Jonah,* 221.

to God?  Rather, in Jonah 4:11, God presents that it contains 120,000 souls who were ignorant of Him.

One might note, this time when commanding Jonah to go, God does not tell Jonah to "cry against it; for their wickedness" (Jonah 1:2).  Instead, God commands that Jonah is to "preach unto it the preaching that I bid thee" (Jonah 3:2).  All the while, God had been preparing the people of Nineveh to hear His word.

John Hannah wrote in the *Bible Knowledge Commentary*: "Before Jonah arrived at this seemingly impregnable fortress-city, two plagues had erupted there (in 765 and 759 B.C.) and a total eclipse of the sun occurred on June 15, 763.  These were considered signs of divine anger."[25] Furthermore, the story of Jonah's plight with the sailors, the magnitude of the storm, and God's calming of the storm most likely preceded Jonah's arrival.

Some say that Jonah's skin was bleached from the acid in the fish's stomach, giving credence to the fish story. But, that part is merely speculation and has no place of verification.

## An Obedient Servant (3:3-4)

Whereas, Jonah previously got up to run in the opposite direction, this time he gets up and heads toward Nineveh. Although, he is obedient; there is no indication that he goes with an obedient

---

[25] Hannah, "Jonah", 1462.

heart. As Rabbi Bob notes, "Jonah does not say a word to either of God's calls."[26] He compares Jonah's lack of response to the response of Abraham, when asked to go to Mt. Moriah to sacrifice his son. "Abraham responds, *"Hineni"* or "Here I am."[27] Not Jonah. He doesn't say a word.

*"Hineni"* is the same response given by Moses and is the word used by Isaiah years later when speaking to the children in exile in Isaiah 58:9, referring to God's response when they turn to seek Him. It means: "I am here, fully engaged, totally yours."

---

[26] Bob, *Jonah,* 149.
[27] Ibid.

Rabbi Bob goes on to write: "I believe that Jonah never recites this key declaration of presence, *hineni,* because he is never as fully present to God as Abraham and Moses were. Jonah goes to Nineveh to fulfill his mission, but he has not fully committed himself to God's cause."[28]

Critics present the size of Nineveh as a point of controversy to discredit the authenticity of Jonah, where the scripture reports that Nineveh was an "exceeding great city of three days journey" (Jonah 3:3). Yet, as the Liberty Bible Commentary presents, the size of Nineveh is "an aggregate of three cities, including Nineveh in the center"[29] much like the metropolitan areas of any city today

---

[28] Bob, *Jonah,* 150.
[29] Falwell, *Liberty,* 1331.

including a larger area. In addition to this first explanation, Hannah goes further to say, "taking three days to go through such a city and its suburbs is reasonable since Jonah stopped and preached along the way."[30]

Jonah's message was simple, "Yet forty days, and Nineveh shall be overthrown" (Jonah 3:4). Of interesting note, Rabbi Bob writes that the word *nehpachet* translated here as overthrown should be overturned.

"A more literal translation of *nehpachet* is 'overturned.'"[31] This translation leaves it more ambiguous, in that either the Ninevites repent and

---

[30] Hannah, "Jonah", 1463.
[31] Bob, *Jonah*, 151

their hearts are overturned or if not, they will be overturned (overthrown). Rabbi Bob further quotes Lamentations 1:20 as further evidence confirming this translation as being overturned, "My heart has turned over within me, *nehpach libi b'kirbi*"[32] Therefore, by God instructing Jonah to preach, saying these words; either way the prophecy will be fulfilled.

## Revival Comes to Nineveh (3:5-10)

The scripture reports, "So the people of Nineveh believed God, and proclaimed a fast and put on sackcloth, from the greatest of them even to the least of them" (Jonah 3:5). This again closely parallels the events regarding the sailors in chapter

---

[32] Bob, *Jonah*, 152.

1, where the sailors had responded with first an internal faith response of both mind and heart; followed by a vocal proclamation, and finally an external response of obedient faith.

Both the sailors and the Ninevites demonstrate God's universality of salvation for both gentile and Jew. An inward action of belief, a vocal acknowledgement, and an outward demonstration of what has occurred through faith. The word spread quickly and when the king of Nineveh heard, he also repented. Robert Chisholm writes: "When the news reached the king, he exchanged his royal robes for sackcloth and issued a proclamation that all people and animals should fast, wear sackcloth, cry out to God, and, most importantly, abandon their evil behavior (vv. 6-8)."[33] This was an acknowledgement that Yahweh, the God of Israel was the only true God. He is, was, and will always be the only way for gentiles and Jews to be saved (Isaiah 45:22, 49:6, 52:10). All the Jewish rituals and sacrifices were worthless without hearts that truly worshipped God as Yahweh. (Psalm 40:6-7, Hosea 9:4, Amos 5:24-26).

Furthermore, in both the case of the sailors and that of the Ninevites they had hope that God might be gracious and suspend His judgement. "Who can tell if God will turn and repent, and turn away from his fierce anger, that we perish not?"

---

[33] Robert B. Chisholm, Jr., *Handbook of the Prophets,* (Grand Rapids, MI: Baker Academic, 2002), 413.

(Jonah 3:9). The sailors had bid Jonah to pray, "if so be that God will think upon us, that we not perish" (Jonah 1:6). Their hope was also a demonstration of faith. "Faith is the substance of things hoped for, the evidence of things not seen" (Hebrews 11:1).

Then, God sees the change of heart of the Ninevite people; and, does not bring judgement upon the people of Nineveh. Sheri Klouda wrote in Baker Illustrated Bible: "Significantly, the Lord recognizes not the outward expression of Nineveh's contrition but the city's willingness to renounce wickedness and evil. (3:10)."[34] Because, He saw their true hearts of repentance, God "repented of the

---

[34] Klouda, *Baker Bible Commentary,* "The Lord Relents from Judgement".

evil that he had said that he would do unto them; and he did it not" (Jonah 3:10). Some scholars and critics use this to try to say that God can be swayed to change His mind; however, that cannot be true.

God is omniscient, and His word is always faithful and true. There are many scriptures to confirm God does not "repent" as humans do (Psalms 110:4, Ezekiel 24:14). All that He has planned, He will accomplish (Isaiah 46:3-11). Remember the discussion earlier regarding the specific wording of "overturned." Certainly, the entire lifestyle of the Ninevites was overturned. The prophecy was fulfilled; although, later generations of Ninevites would return to their evil ways. 150 years later Nahum would prophecy of their destruction; however, they did not heed God's warning the next time and they were destroyed.

God has at times used the word "repent" or "repented" when He has delayed a judgement or when discussing the evil nature of mankind causing Him to "repent of having created man"; however, in these cases His wording is only to reach out in a manner that we might grasp the depth of His hatred of sin or to demonstrate His abundance of grace. In no way, does this indicate that God changed His mind.

He is never taken by surprise and knows everything before it happens. He knew the response of the Ninevites, before He commissioned Jonah to go. And He knew His response to their repentance.

Yet, to explain this to the finite human mind; He uses terms at times to explain events that can help the human mind and heart to understand. As Sheri Klouda wrote:

> We can only understand the author's choice of words as an attempt to grapple with the inconceivability of God's restraint from judgment in light of his divine holiness. The incomprehensible nature and will of God is expressed in terms that ascribe human qualities to the divine being in order to explain God's actions within the limitations of human concepts. [35]

Furthermore, it is necessary to interpret the use of the word "repent" by considering other scripture. Since scripture interprets scripture, we

---

[35] Klouda, *Baker Bible Commentary,* "The Lord Relents from Judgement".

must look at the whole of scripture before coming to conclusions regarding an isolated verse.

As noted in Numbers 23:19: "God is not a man, that He should lie; neither the son of man, that He should repent: hath He said, and shall He not do it? Or hath He spoken, and shall He not make it good?" One must only look through the corridors of time to see that God always fulfilled every promise. Jesus rode into Jerusalem on the exact day prophesied by Daniel (Daniel 9:26), fulfilling much of Isaiah's prophecy as well. The Babylonian exiles were restored. The temple and wall rebuilt, exactly as prophesied. Therefore, God's usage of the word translated "repented", had a very distinct purpose and in no way was meant to change the truth of

God's Sovereignty, Omniscience and Steadfast fulfillment of all that He has planned.

As a final thought for this book, concerning this use of repent, consider these truths. There are mysteries regarding God that may seem hard to understand in our finiteness; and others, will remain shrouded in mystery until one day we stand before Him in eternity.

An example of that is. God calls upon mankind to pray, just as He calls upon mankind to repent of their sins; providing free will. Does the course of events change because of mankind's prayers? C. S. Lewis wrote in depth about prayer in his *Letters to Malcolm.* Therein, Lewis questioned the purpose of prayer addressing that very question as to whether it changes the course of things. If God already knows what will happen does our prayer change things at all? In his conclusions, Lewis recognized that the necessity of our praying and God's Sovereignty were not at enmity with each other. Rather, both were equally true.

You see, God is not bound by time and space as we know it. The fact that God sees fully all that will happen, does not diminish the moment one cries out to Him nor does it diminish free will of mankind to choose Him. Although the prayer of the Ninevites changed the course in that **moment of time**, God's omniscience already knew that they would repent and pray; therefore, He did not change.

Our desperate, fervent prayer in any moment in time does not go unheard or unanswered by Almighty God. His miraculous response is within that moment in time; yet, his answering our prayer does not diminish His Eternal Sovereignty and Omniscience. As He said, "If my people, which are called by my name, shall humble themselves, and pray, and seek my face, and turn from their wicked ways; then will I hear from heaven, and will forgive their sin, and will heal their land" (2 Chronicles 7:14). In that moment, His response is here and now. His grace is poured forth at that moment in time. His pleas are no less sincere nor less passionate in His love toward each of us, even when He knows that the response of some will be rejection of His plea.

Again, all this perhaps is a mystery our feeble minds cannot fully comprehend. Yet, our inability to comprehend it, does not change its truth. Rather, that is where faith steps in to fill the gap. I have seen His miraculous answer to my feeblest of prayers. If you have walked with Him any length of time, I am sure you have seen the same. Does that lessen His Sovereignty over every detail of my life? No.

How He can take all my brokenness and even my failures, cover them with the righteousness of Christ and then use them for His Glory once I have laid them at His feet with a broken and contrite heart will always be a mystery to me. Yet, that mystery draws my heart ever closer to His, wherein I find rest and comfort for my soul. Therein, drawn near to His heart, He teaches me to love Him better and stronger as I surrender to His Will, trusting Him with every minute detail of my life.

## Lessons from God (Chapter 4)

After having saved the sailors and the Ninevites, God would now turn to deal with His angry prophet. Although, God had been dealing with Jonah from the very beginning; now He would address Jonah's unforgiving heart. Despite the grace afforded him repeatedly by God, Jonah still did not understand. Somehow, he saw himself as deserving of grace; whereas, he believed the Ninevites were not. Neither did Jonah realize that God's plan was best for him, and the Israel nation as well.

The only other prophecy recorded of Jonah was one of grace toward Israel. II Kings 14:25 records that Jeroboam II had expanded the kingdom

Israel as prophesied "by the hand of his servant Jonah." This prophecy was graciously fulfilled despite the truth that Jeroboam II was an evil king "who made Israel to sin." Beyond that, we know little of Jonah's spiritual life. Certainly, he would not want to return to Israel as the "one who saved Nineveh." His reputation was on the line. He had believed it ok to extend a prophecy of grace to the evil king that lead Israel to sin. But whose sin was worse, the nation of Israel who blatantly sinned despite all that God had revealed to them and done for them or Nineveh who sinned in ignorance of God?

Furthermore, many of the prophets in Israel during the time of Jeroboam II were corrupt as well.

Was Jonah's faith all confounded with theirs? The prophets at that time were so corrupt that God had called a shepherd, Amos, to be His prophet to the people. It is rather clear that until now, Jonah's theology was at least, a little mixed up. Jonah did not consider that this act of grace toward the Ninevites was also grace toward Israel, whose invasion by the Assyrians was postponed by more than 130 years.

After, extending His grace to Nineveh, God now would reach out once more to Jonah. God did not leave Jonah there in his confused, mixed up state. Instead, God reached out to His servant with patience and kindness. God's pursuing love seeking to help His wayward child to grasp the heighth, depth, and width of God's grace toward him.

**An Unjustly Angry Servant (4:1-4)**

Jonah was furious that God would save these gentiles. In his anger, he bitterly complains to God, quoting God's own words back to him. He refers to God's description of Himself to Moses in Exodus 34:6-7: "The Lord God, merciful and gracious, long-suffering, and abundant in goodness and truth, keeping mercy for thousands, forgiving iniquity and transgression and sin." Yet, in his quote, he fails to complete the sentence; although, he does seem to be thinking it. "and will by no means clear the guilty." In Jonah's eyes, these Ninevites were the guilty and God was unjust in forgiving them. God had proclaimed in one sentence both His great mercy at "forgiving iniquity and transgression and sin"; while at the same time proclaiming His justice in not clearing the "guilty." Who then are the "guilty?" Certainly, Jonah saw himself as deserving of God's gracious forgiveness. However, he believed the Ninevites were not.

Moses upon hearing God's words "made haste, and bowed his head toward the earth, and worshiped" repenting of the sins of the "stiffnecked people" he was leading, pleading for God to pardon theirs and his "iniquity and sin" (Exodus 34:8-9). Just as Joel had clearly written in Joel 2:12-14:

> "Therefore, also now, saith the Lord, turn ye even to me with all your heart, and with fasting, and with weeping, and with mourning: and rend

your heart, and not your garments, and turn unto the Lord your God: for he is gracious and merciful, slow to anger and of great kindness, and repenteth him of the evil. Who knoweth if he will return and repent and leave a blessing behind him."

Moses and Joel clearly understood that God's mercy was given to those who had truly repentant hearts. The truly guilty in this case was Jonah and the Israelite nation, who to this point, had not bowed in repentance; whereas, the Ninevites had. Jonah was fully representative of the Israelites to whom he ultimately wrote this prophecy. They felt because of "who they were as Jews" they deserved God's mercy; even though they were the guilty, unrepentant ones.

As the Liberty Bible Commentary presents: "Jonah still maintains a false Jewish nationalism and hatred of all non-Jews, especially Assyrians"[36] Because at this point, Jonah does not yet understand the truth of God's grace and justice, he goes so far as to say his own disobedience was justified.

Philip Stern pinpoints this: "In other words, the outcome of Jonah's prophecy is such that he feels secure in telling God that he was justified in the first place for fleeing to Tarshish."[37] His anger was so great, that he asked God to take his life. He would rather die than to live with the thought that God would show grace to the Ninevites or to face

---

[36] Falwell, *Liberty,* 1332.

[37] Philip Stern, "Jonah, the miserable prophet." *Midstream 57,* no. 4 (2011), 24.

the criticism of the Nation of Israel when he returned home.

He would be considered by his Jewish peers a disgrace; because, they too were so steeped in ritual without having repentant hearts for their sins against God. They too felt they were deserving of God's mercy and grace; just because.

God does not lecture Jonah, nor try to reason with him; instead, He asks of Jonah one question, "Doest thou well to be angry?" (Jonah 4:4). As John MacArthur writes, "Jonah's anger was kindled because his will did not prevail; rather God's will did."[38] So, Jonah went out east of the city to sit and watch what might become of the city.

---

[38] MacArthur, *Bible Commentary,* 1012.

Did he think his anger might change God's mind or did he still believe he was right? Sheri Klouda wrote: "Jonah travels east of Nineveh and settles down to wait for Nineveh's demise, as if it is inconceivable that the city would be spared by God."[39] Obviously, his theology and understanding of God was still upside down.

## Lessons from a Gourd (4:5-9)

Despite Jonah's irrational behavior, his unrepentant heart, and his blatant anger toward God, God graciously causes a gourd to grow up and provide comforting shade for His prophet. Jonah was "exceedingly glad of the gourd" (4:6). Early

---

[39] Klouda, *Baker Bible Commentary,* "God's Response to Jonah's Unjustified Anger".

the next day, God sent a worm to destroy the gourd. Then God sent a fierce hot wind which with the sun beating down brought great distress to Jonah. God was Sovereign over the gourd, the worm, the fierce hot wind, and the sun. Once more Jonah was furious, wanting to die.

Again, God questions Jonah concerning his anger, "Doest thou well to be angry for the gourd?" (Jonah 4:9). This time instead of walking away, Jonah replies, "I do well to be angry, even unto death" (4:9). God replies, "You have pity on the gourd, for the which thou has not labored, neither madest it grow, which came up in a night and perished in a night: And should not I spare Nineveh, that great city, wherein are more than six score thousand persons that cannot discern between their right hand and their left hand" (Jonah 4: 10-11).

As John Hannah wrote:

> God being slow to anger again attempted to reason with Jonah. This time God gave him a visual lesson. God erected an object of Jonah's affection (creaturely comfort) and contrasted it with the object of His own concern (the souls of people). God rebuked Jonah, not through a storm in this instance, but by exposing the selfishness of his likes and dislikes.[40]

God's grace once more shown forth in His patient teaching of His stubborn, selfish prophet, as it had throughout the book of Jonah. Jonah had still not come to the end of himself. He was not fully

---

[40] Hannah, "Jonah", 1471.

surrendered to God as Lord and King; but, God was not finished with Him, yet.

**God's Desire for All to Come (4:10-11)**

In God's final recorded statement to Jonah, He points out that the profound ignorance of the Ninevites by describing them as a people "who did not know their right hand from their left hand." He looked upon them with great compassion and pity; much as Jesus did from the cross years later when he proclaimed, "Father, forgive them for they know not what they do" (Luke 23:34).

Israel had failed in their commission to be an example for the surrounding nations. Ultimately, the Ninevites would turn their back on God and 150 years later they would be overthrown by the

Babylonians; however, before that God's light did shine down into a generation. He made certain, before they denied Him, they were given the chance to know Him.

So, what happened to Jonah? The recording of the story ends there. However, despite it making him look a fool, he did write the story and presented it to the stubborn Israelites. He ultimately did stand as one of the prophets, for his people, urging them to repentance at the risk of his own humiliation. His story is read every year at Yom Kippur, symbolizing the truth that true worship comes from a humble, repentant heart of love and gratitude. Jonah exemplified the opposite; however, in doing so pointed to the truth of God's pursuing Grace and Glory.

Jonah's writing of this book stands out as an example of ultimate surrender to God's will; otherwise, he would have never written the humiliating truth. Never could the proud and arrogant Jonah tell this embarrassing story of himself, unless he had come to the end of himself, where God's victory can be found.

It also demonstrates God's relentless pursuit of Jonah's heart. God's grace pursued Jonah, his mercy engulfed him, and ultimately His Love transformed him into one man surrendered fully to God's will. That was when this "minor prophet" became the prophet for all the ages. Not only to his people, but to the whole world, even today.

Jesus even spoke of Jonah by name. God's grace toward Jonah had been longsuffering through the time of his own unrepentance. Perhaps, God also had seen his ignorance of the truth, as He did the Ninevites.

Ah, but the truth is: Jonah is the story of God's relentless pursuit of the sinner, while at the same time displaying His Grace, His mercy and His Sovereignty.

We are all so much like Jonah, wanting to follow God on our terms, placing Him in a box of our own making. I thank God, He did not give up on Jonah, nor did He give up on me. My question to you is: "Have you come to the end of yourself and surrendered yourself to the only way of salvation? Have you accepted Jesus Christ as Your Lord and Savior, leaving all else in pursuit of Him?"

God is longsuffering, merciful and gracious; but, He is also righteous and just. He paid the price that we might be saved. He bids you to come; but, just as the later generations of the Ninevites were destroyed when they returned to their evil ways, judgment will come one day. That it has not yet come, is because God's grace is waiting still for one more sinner to come to Him. But judgment will come suddenly in an instant when God's trumpets sound.

As God wrote in Deuteronomy 32:34

*To me belongeth vengeance and recompence: (the unrepentant sinner who failed to accept Jesus Christ as their Savior by faith in Him), their foot shall slide in due time: for the day of their calamity is at hand, and the things that shall come upon them make haste.*

## Applications for Life

APPLICATION #1.

Jonah was commanded by God to "Arise and go to Nineveh" (Jonah 1:2). Yet, Jonah disobeyed God and faced the consequences of his disobedience. At the same time, the Israelite nation to whom Jonah prophesied were commanded of God to awaken from their spiritual sleep and obey God. If not, there would be consequences. However, if they obeyed and turned their hearts to God; they would be blessed.

Christians are commanded to be beacons of light by example and speech to a world filled with darkness, just as Israel had been commanded (Isaiah 49:3, 60:1-3). God through Paul in Ephesians 5:1-2, 14-16, commands the same of us, *"Be ye therefore followers of God, as dear children; and walk in love as Christ also hath loved us, and hath given himself for us an offering and a sacrifice to God for a sweet smelling savour...Wherefore he saith, Awake thou that sleepest, and arise from the dead, and Christ shall give thee light. See then that ye walk circumspectly, not as fools, but as wise, redeeming the time, because the days are evil."*

This command to us as stewards of the gospel message directly reflects the command given to Jonah to "Arise" and that in Isaiah 60 to the Jewish nation, *"Arise, shine; for thy light is come, and the glory of the Lord is risen upon thee. For behold, the darkness shall cover the earth, and gross darkness the people: but, the Lord shall arise upon thee, and His glory shall be seen upon thee. And the Gentiles shall come to thy light, and kings to the brightness of thy rising.*"

We as Christians are commissioned to be lights in the world. Either we obey God's command and receive the blessings of God's joy and glory or we face the consequences of our disobedience in bitterness, anger, and sorrow.

APPLICATION #2:

God did not need Jonah to save the sailors, nor the Ninevites, for that matter. He commissioned Jonah as an act of grace toward Jonah. God did not need the Israelites to accomplish His plans, either. Again, His covenant with Abraham was an act of His Sovereign love and grace. The Israelites had failed to understand this.

God choosing Israel to be His covenant people and to be the lineage to which He brought forth His plan of salvation had been an act of His grace. Jesus commissioned the church to go into all the world to preach the gospel (Mark 16:15).

This, again, is an act of God's Sovereign Grace. *"God that made the world and all things therein, seeing that he is Lord of heaven and*

*earth dwelleth not in temples made with hands;*
*Neither is worshiped with men's hands, as*
*though He needed anything, seeing He giveth to*
*all life, and breath, and all things"* (Acts 17:24-
25).

When God allows the testimony of a believer
to be used in the salvation of a soul, He is
pouring out His gracious love upon that
believer. In thus doing, He is sharing with them
a piece of His glory, not because they deserve
such grace, rather because of His love for them.
That is what Jesus presented in John 17: 22-23:
*"And the glory which thou gavest me I have*
*given them; that they may be one, even as we are*
*one: I in them, and thou in me, that they may be*

*made perfect in one; and that the world may know that thou hast sent me, and has loved them, as thou has loved me."*

Every Christian should recognize that it is a privilege to be a testimony for Christ to the world. It must come, not as some act of duty to gain brownie points, rather, as an overflowing of love for Jesus Christ and knowing this is a privilege given by God's grace, not a task to be performed. Flowing forth from that privilege is abounding love and joy for the believer. What joy should fill our hearts, when we witness the eternity of one soul being saved. Even more so, when God has used us as His instrument of Grace, realizing He didn't need us; but, He used us anyway. He allowed us to share in His gospel message and glory, as underserving as we are.

APPLICATION #3:

When drowning in the sea, Jonah's eyes turned toward God as his only hope. The nation of Israel, while enjoying relative prosperity, had not turned to look to God. Yet, when they would soon find themselves in the belly of captivity with the life of their nation nearly snuffed out, some would cry out to the only one who could save them. Only then would they reach the point that they would turn their eyes to God once more. As in Psalm 107: 25-31:

> "For He (God) commandeth, and raiseth the stormy wind, which lifteth up the waves thereof. They mount up

to the heaven, they go down again to the depths: their soul is melted because of trouble. They reel to and for, and stagger like a drunken man, and are at their wit's end. Then they cry unto the Lord in their trouble, and he bringeth them out of their distresses. He maketh the storm a calm, so that the waves thereof are still. Then are they glad because they be quiet; so he bring them unto their desired haven. Of that men would praise the Lord for his goodness, and for his wonderful works to the children of men!"

Even if God sends the storm to enlarge our faith, or He hurls the storm due to our disobedience, or we find ourselves in a storm of our own making, when we turn to cry out to Him, He calms the storm. God is more interested in transforming our hearts, so we might discover true joy in Him, than He is with our daily comfort in counterfeit joys that will never fully satisfy. It is comforting to know He always hears the cries of His children for help when they turn to call on Him.

*The righteous cry, and the Lord heareth, and delivereth them out of all their troubles. The Lord is night unto them that are of a broken heart; and saveth such as be of a contrite spirit. Many are the afflictions of the righteous: but the Lord delivereth him out of them all.* (Psalm 34:17-19).

APPLICATION #4:

Jonah is given a second chance to obey God's command (Jonah 3:1-2), after having failed God through his disobedience. The nation of Israel and Judah are given many chances to repent.

Yet, they did not heed the warnings of the prophets and would face exile. The northern kingdom would be overtaken by the Assyrians in 722 B.C. and the Southern Kingdom by the Babylonians in 586 B. C. Despite all that, God promised to restore a remnant of true believers to Jerusalem and promises to bring them again one day in the future to a place of righteousness where his laws are written upon their hearts.

Within the New Testament, John Mark failed in his missionary journey and turned back. Yet, he was restored as a missionary. Ultimately, he wrote the gospel of Mark with his missionary work continuing today through the gospel message. It is comforting to know that God is a

God of second chances. He does not give up on His children; in fact, He promises to complete the work He began in us (Philippians 1:6). Jesus is "the author and the finisher of our faith" (Hebrews 12:2). Disobedience brings grave consequences, but out of that, God brings forth purified gold (I Peter 6:7). How much easier to obey the first time God commands!

APPLICATION #5:

God goes to great lengths to demonstrate to Jonah the truth of His grace and justice. The Israelite nation much like Jonah, believed God's grace toward them would stand because of His covenant with them, regardless of their hearts being unrepentant for their sins. They took His grace for granted, ignoring their own evil hearts.

As God revealed to Jeremiah:

> *At what instant I shall speak concerning a nation, and concerning a kingdom, to pluck up, and to pull down, and to destroy it; if that nation, against whom I have pronounced, turn from their evil, I will repent of the evil that I thought to do unto them. And at what instant I shall speak concerning a nation, and concerning a kingdom, to build and to plant it; If it do evil in my sight, that it obey not my voice, then I will repent of the good, wherewith I said I would benefit them* (Jeremiah 18:7-10).

God was revealing to Jonah and the nation of Israel the truth of His nature as presented in Exodus 34:6-7: "*The Lord God, merciful and gracious, long-suffering, and abundant in goodness and truth, keeping mercy for thousands, forgiving iniquity and transgression and sin, and will by no means clear the guilty."*

The same is true today. Often, people speak flippantly of God's Grace and love without considering His Righteous, Just nature. Grace is poured out upon those who come to Him with a broken, contrite heart of repentance. His justice stands against the guilty. Whom are the guilty? Those who fail to acknowledge their sin and come to the foot of the cross, repenting of their sin and believing that Jesus Christ is their only hope of salvation.

APPLICATION #6:

We are commissioned to go into all the world and preach the gospel (Mark 16:15). I am not given the option to preach the gospel only to those whom I think are worthy to be saved. As Paul wrote in Romans 9:15-16, quoting Exodus 33:19, *"For He saith to Moses, I will have mercy on whom I will have mercy, and I will have compassion on whom I will have compassion. So, then it is not of him that willeth, nor of him that runneth, but of God that sheweth mercy."*

Only when I fully recognize that I am guilty before a holy God, undeserving of the marvelous Grace He has shown me, can I demonstrate that same Grace and Mercy to all. My commission is to present the gospel message to everyone I meet. I am no worthier of His grace than another. My salvation came by grace alone. He wooed me, He called me, and He pursued me. If there is anything good within me, it comes from His Grace pouring out in and through me. No one is too far gone to be outside of God's reach. I am to pray for them and witness of His Grace, Mercy and Love through my actions and my words. My commission is to tell all whom I meet of the good news of the gospel.

APPLICATION #7:

God will never leave me where He found me. He doesn't just save me from eternal separation from Him. He also transforms me from the inside out. Sometimes that means I must go through storms, be blasted with the hot winds in the desert heat, or face trials so harsh that if He doesn't save me, I will die. But His promise is that He will save me, He will transform me step by step into the image of Christ (Romans 8:29). Only when I come to the end of me can I find victory in Jesus Christ. There is no refuge apart from God there is only refuge in God through faith in Jesus Christ.

# Grace So Grand

My Lord, how can I understand
The Grace on which my faith doth stand?
A Grace so grand that sought me out
Pursued this heart so filled with doubt

My heart desired for lesser things
Like love of men or diamond rings
And though I did not seek your face
You reached to me to give me grace

How could it be you loved me so?
That on this heart of stone bestow
A love so great it drew me in
And pardoned me for all my sin

Forgiving all that I have done
Redeemed I stand by thy dear Son
That died the death that should be mine
So, in His Glory I might shine

As beacon of His love so pure
Tis Grace that holds my heart secure
Your Grace that drew my heart aside
And bid me in your love abide

And by thy Grace my heart doth vow
To give you all, before you bow
My life is yours-do as you will
What e'er it takes to this heart fill

With your dear love, to overflow
Unto the world that they may know
It was your Grace that loved me so
Your joy has set my life a glow

Your Grace does call to them to come

Drawn by your love to then succumb

Unto your will, accept your Son

And know the life that He hath won

# BIBLIOGRAPHY

Allen, Leslie. *The Books of Joel, Obadiah, Jonah, and Micah. (The New International Commentary on the Old Testament).* eds. Harrison, R.K and Robert Hubbard, Jr. Grand Rapids, MI: Wm B. Eerdsmans Publishing, 1976.

Bob, Steven. *Jonah and the Meaning of Our Lives: A Verse-by-Verse Contemporary Commentary,* The Jewish Publication Society, 2016

Chisholm, Jr., Robert B. *Handbook of the Prophets,* Grand Rapids, MI: Baker Academic, 2002.

Falwell, Jerry, ed. *The Liberty Annotated Study Bible.* Nashville, TN: Thomas Nelson,1988.

Hannah, John D. "Jonah". *The Bible Knowledge Commentary: An Exposition of the Scriptures by Dallas Seminary Faculty-Old Testament*, eds. John F. Woovard and Roy B. Zuck. Colorado Springs, CO: Victor, 2004. 1461-1473.

Klouda, Sheri L. "Jonah." In *Baker Illustrated Bible Commentary*, by Gary M. Burge, and Andrew E. Hill. 2nd ed. Baker Publishing Group, 2012.

MacArthur, John. *The MacArthur Bible Commentary.* Nashville, TN: Thomas Nelson, 2005.

Stern, Philip. "Jonah, the miserable prophet." *Midstream 57,* no. 4 (2011):23+